Finely Feathered

David Lynch

Finely Feathered

The Marsh and Lagoon Birds of the Lowcountry

David Lynch

HILTON HEAD ISLAND

BEAUFORT

THE SEA ISLANDS

CHARLESTON

SAVANNAH

A keen observer of the natural world, DAVID LYNCH began his photography career as an aerial photographer and pilot. Prior to following his passion for the wild outdoors, David was a high school biology teacher for 30 years. As a lifelong educator, he prepared brief lessons for people to read as they observed his wildlife photographs. The positive feedback encouraged him to compile the photographs and information about the beautiful marsh and lagoon birds of the Lowcountry and prepare *Finely Feathered* for your enjoyment. He resides on the sea islands of South Carolina.

Finely Feathered *The Marsh and Lagoon Birds of the Lowcountry*

Copyright © 2011 by David Lynch

ISBN: 978-0-9831519-1-3

All rights reserved. No portion of this book may be reproduced, stored in a retrieval system, or transmitted in any form or by any means—mechanical, electronic, photocopying, recording, or otherwise—without prior written permission from the publisher, except as provided by United States of America copyright law. Printed in China.

Published by Lydia Inglett Ltd.
www.lydiainglett.com

To order more copies of this book contact:
David Lynch
92 Barony Lane
Hilton Head Island, SC 29928
843-342-3637
dlynch43@roadrunner.com

Find us on Facebook

Or, order securely online at www.lowcountrybirds.com and www.starbooks.biz

Dedication

Finely Feathered is dedicated to my wife, Carolee, who gave me the encouragement and support needed to accomplish this book. She demonstrated extreme patience while she accompanied me on many photography trips and while I edited the photographs and prepared the text. During this time she also had the unselfish desire to volunteer for an Alzheimer's drug research trial in hopes that knowledge will be gained quickly, so that others, in the future, will not have to live with this disease as she has courageously done for many years.

CONTENTS

Introduction	8
Herons	**14**
Great Blue Heron	16
Little Blue Heron	24
Tricolored Heron	30
Green Heron	38
Black-crowned Night Heron	42
Yellow-crowned Night Heron	48

Egrets	**52**
Snowy Egret	54
Great Egret	62
Ibis	**72**
White Ibis	74
Glossy Ibis	80

Rails	**84**
King Rail	86
Clapper Rail	88
American Coot	90
Common Moorhen	96
Wilson's Snipe	**100**

Killdeer	104
Spotted Sandpiper	108
Wood Stork	110
Double-crested Cormorant	118
Anhinga	124
Belted Kingfisher	130
Ducks	134
Ring-necked Duck	136
Wood Duck	140
Canvasback Duck	142
Redhead Duck	144
Ruddy Duck	148
Lesser Scaup	150
Hooded Merganser	152
Bufflehead	156
Pied-billed Grebe	160
Osprey	162
Bald Eagle	168
References	176

Introduction

WALKING, JOGGING or biking along one of the many beautiful beaches in the Lowcountry, you may see quite a variety of interesting wildlife. Dolphins may be breaking the surface to get a breath before submerging to continue their hunt for fish. Pelicans may be enjoying their fresh catch obtained by diving into the surf for fish they have spotted from high above the ocean's surface. Sandpipers, plovers and crabs scurry just out of reach of the playing children. Gulls will not miss an opportunity to get a free meal from people picnicking at the shore. Using their superb sense of vision and smell they will have no difficulty locating food.

Striking examples of migrating shore birds are visible to those fortunate to be at the beach at the proper time of the year.

However, did you know there is an entirely different group of plants and animals living away from the beach and found in the marshes and lagoons that make up much of the Lowcountry's topography?

The purpose of this book is to show you birds that inhabit these marshes and lagoons. There are many excellent field guides that provide information about bird species. That is not the main purpose of this book. Instead, it is designed to allow everyone the chance to enjoy the beauty of these marvelous birds any time of the year.

Marbled Godwit

Brown Pelican

Willets

Royal Tern

American Oyster Catcher

Ruddy Turnstone

THE LOWCOUNTRY refers to the region along the Atlantic coast that extends from Charleston south into Georgia. This area was formed as the continental shelf when the east coast was under water. The many rivers that empty into the Atlantic Ocean carried sediments that were deposited as the river currents slowed when they reached the ocean. Over time these sediments formed a thick, fairly level layer along the coast. Due to climate changes and geologic forces that raised the region the Lowcountry was formed as the ocean waters receded. Low areas became our current marshes while elevated land became our many "Sea Islands" as well as the level dry land that now extends well inland.

These marshes and both natural and constructed lagoons provide the home for the birds that you will see and read about. Hopefully you will have the opportunity to observe them for yourself in their natural surroundings as well.

We are fortunate that we have the opportunity to enjoy these photographs and see these Lowcountry birds because most of them were brought to near extinction more than one hundred years ago. From the late 1800s into the early 1900s women's feathered hats had become a worldwide fashion sensation. The once very large populations of many species of marsh and lagoon birds were nearly eliminated when millions of birds were killed to meet the demand for feathers. Ironically, it was people's interest and admiration of nature and its beauty that brought about this craze. Women wanted to be close to nature and believed that by wearing these feathered hats they were demonstrating their interest and excitement about its beauty.

More than two dozen Gull species may be seen along the Lowcountry coast at different times of the year. Their niche, or role in nature, is to act as scavengers and eat nearly anything dead or dying, or your picnic lunch if you are not looking.

Ring-billed Gull

Fortunately, a few individuals had the foresight to anticipate the dire consequences if the bird population destruction continued and rallied against the killing and saved many species from extinction. Can we learn from this? Have we? I sure hope so.

FIELD GUIDES LIST over two thousand species of North American birds which are generally grouped into sixty two categories based on their appearance and behavior. I will show those whose niche is the Lowcountry's marshes and lagoons. That is, these birds survive by getting the majority of their food from the plants and animals that also live in these watery habitats. Other birds such as Marsh Wrens and Red Winged Black Birds also live in the marshes, but they do not depend on obtaining food from the water so are not included here.

Some of these birds can be seen frequently while others are rarely seen. Some stay most of the year while others make brief visits as they migrate along their coastal flyways.

You will read a brief narrative about each of the birds pictured and I hope this will stimulate you to seek more information as well as motivate you to look and see how many of these marvelous birds you can find, not at the beach where you may see the birds I've shown in this introduction, but in the marshes and lagoons of the beautiful Lowcountry.

Cool morning air causes the warm moisture over the marsh to condense and form fog. Beauty and serenity to start the day.

HERONS

Great Blue Heron

Little Blue Heron

Tricolored Heron

Green Heron

Black-crowned Night Heron

Yellow-crowned Night Heron

This stately, quiet bird is a stealthy hunter, often standing still and silently watching for his next meal of fish.

Great Blue Heron
Ardea herodias

How tall are you? Did you know that if you stretch your arms straight out to the side, your 'arm span' is the same as your height? Well, the tallest of the marsh and lagoon birds of the Lowcountry is the Great Blue Heron, which stands as tall as 46 inches, but has a wing span of nearly seven feet.

The herons are grouped together because they are the long legged waders. The largest heron in the Lowcountry is the Great Blue Heron; they are usually easy to find because of their size and the fact that they stay in this area for most of the year. Great Blue Herons survive by wading into inland waters and patiently waiting for fish to come within reach. Along with the long legs, they also possess long necks and beaks to make their hunting as practical as possible.

As you will learn, each species has adapted a different approach to its eating technique so that competition is mini-

The largest of all herons, The Great Blue Heron is as majestic on land as it is in flight.

The male Great Blue Heron presents a stick to the female. Just one part of the complex mating ritual. If she accepts his gift, together they will begin work on their nest construction.

When young, the chicks will remain very still and quiet, but as they get a little older they will watch every bird in flight to see if their next meal is being delivered.

mized. Obviously, the tallest, the Great Blue, is able to fish in the deeper waters. With a quick lunge, these birds capture food in their beaks and deftly maneuver their prey for quick and easy swallowing. If food is plentiful in deeper water, the Great Blue Heron may hover over the water and reach the fish with the movement of its head and neck. These birds have even been observed diving into the water to catch a meal, but this is not common.

Many Great Blue Herons stay in the Lowcountry during the spring mating season. The male starts the nesting behavior by

presenting the female with a nest building stick. At the completion of the nest building, or repair of one from the previous year, the female will accept the male's invitation to join him. She will soon lay three to six eggs, which both parents will share in incubating for 28 days.

After hatching, the chicks will stay quite inactive and will lie in the nest, still and quiet, except for when a parent returns to the nest with food. After about two weeks, the young will become more active and curious about their surroundings. Of course, awaiting the next meal is one of their main activities.

As you will learn, many of the birds that live in the Lowcountry's waters share the care and feeding of their young. When one Great Blue Heron returns to relieve its partner and feed the chicks, there is frequently a ritual displaying of the

The adult Great Blue Herons carry on a brief greeting display as one returns to the nest to relieve the other. There is no sign of food for the chicks because it will be regurgitated from the parent directly into the chick's mouth.

The Lowcountry is an ideal breeding sanctuary for Great Blue Herons.

Ardea Herodias

The large, powerful wingspan of the Great Blue lets it glide with ease .

Preening is an essential behavior carried out by the marsh and lagoon birds.

'crown' feathers, a signal that it is time to switch parenting duties.

There is no sign that the returning parent is carrying food for the young as is seen with song birds bringing worms or insects back to the nest in their beaks. Because the Great Blue Heron chicks require so much food for their proper growth, the hunting parent swallows a number of fish and then regurgitates them directly into the chick's mouth.

One of the Lowcountry Great Blue Heron pairs had produced only one chick for the past few years, and this trend seemed to continue until a strong late spring storm removed their one chick from the nest. Within a short time, this pair had produced two

chicks to care for late in the nesting season; what a good example of nature's wonders and the adaptability of its wildlife. This probably would not have been possible at the northern extremes of Great Blue Heron breeding grounds, but was possible in the Lowcountry because the chicks still had time to get strong enough to survive the colder months.

Great Blue Heron chicks, as well as many other marsh bird young, have large beaks in proportion to their bodies because their beak is one of the main features which will allow them to survive in their environment. Hopefully, we use our brains to help us survive. We were born with heads that were one quarter of our total length, and as our bodies developed into adulthood, our heads became one seventh of our height. As the Great Blue Heron chick matures, it will soon obtain the proportions we normally observe.

In flight, the Great Blue Heron can appear to be quite massive, but they weigh only 6 to 8 pounds. To remain aerodynamic, the legs point straight back as the heron glides down from the nest to head for the lagoon shore to hunt.

As I was enjoying nature while walking along a narrow tree-lined path in a Lowcountry park, some movement caught my eye. I turned back to see a Great Blue Heron flying toward me. Its head was at the same height as mine and its 7 foot wing span nearly touched the overhanging branches. As it passed, our eyes met, and it gently lifted its left wing so it could pass over my right shoulder. It then raised its right wing to make a sharp left turn so it could follow the path to the water. This brief encounter significantly added to the serenity and beauty of my day at the park.

The Little Blue Heron is an excellent example of how some young Lowcountry marsh and lagoon birds undergo a dramatic change as they mature from juvenile to adult. Right: The blue beak and highlights show that this is not a Snowy Egret, as it may first appear to be, but rather a young Little Blue Heron.

Little Blue Heron
Egretta caerulea

A TRULY BLUE HERON, the Little Blue Heron is not impressive because of its size, at 24 inches, but because of its outstanding coloration. Because of their smaller size, they prefer to stay closer to the shores of the marshes and lagoons where they slowly hunt for fish, shellfish or other available invertebrates.

Both adult Little Blue Herons look the same. The male will select the nesting site and then attract a mate by stretching his beak straight up and swaying his neck while vocalizing or snapping his beak. If the female accepts his invitation, she will entwine her neck with his and share in mutual grooming. They will both build the nest of sticks and grass a few feet above the water level in a shrub or tree. Both parents will incubate the three to five eggs.

In approximately two months, the young are able to leave the nest and start their own hunting. As you will see, many marsh and lagoon bird juveniles look very different from their parents.

The young Little Blue Heron looks more like a Snowy Egret at first, but a close look reveals a blue tint to its beak and the beginning of a bluish cast to its feathers. Soon it will develop the striking blue color on its 41-inch wing span.

Right: You should make an effort to see a Little Blue Heron in nature. Their color can seem to fluctuate not only with seasonal changes at breeding time, but also with the slightest variation in sunlight. Here you see unmistakable evidence of how they got their name.

Below: Where is that long neck required to be classified as a heron? On a cold winter day they do all they can to conserve heat and thus require less food to maintain their body temperature.

Opposite: Then, in the warmth of summer, spreading their 41-inch wings can help radiate heat.

EGRETTA CAERULEA

The Little Blue Heron uses its excellent vision and rapid head and neck movements to capture a variety of prey found living at the marsh edges.

At the same time that bird populations were severely reduced to supply the hat industry with their plumes, egg collecting was also very popular; further reducing bird populations worldwide.

TRICOLORED HERON
Egretta tricolor

Details about the multitude of egg shell colors are still being studied, but it is known that the blue, common to many species, comes from pigments produced by the breakdown of hemoglobin in red blood cells. It is also known that birds see egg coloration differently than humans do.

Unmistakable coloration distinguishes another of the long legged waders. This is aptly named the Tricolored Heron with its blue, white and rust colors making for a very attractive appearance. They are 20 inches shorter than the Great Blue Herons and stand about 26 inches tall. The Tricolored Herons prefer water a little deeper than the shorter herons, but only 7 or 8 inches of water comes up to chest height. Fish is their food preference.

To attract a mate the male will shake a nest building twig, stretch way up with his beak and then collapse downward while vocalizing and displaying his mating plumage. The tan

Two week old chicks show the rapid growth that takes place in this species. By mid-summer they will have developed their flight feathers and be able to hunt for their own food.

tail feathers and blue lores, the coloration in front of the eyes, are mating season developments which will fade as the mating season ebbs. The pair will construct the nest with ever smaller twigs as each layer is completed. A 15 inch nest may not appear sturdy enough to support a 26 inch parent as well as three or four growing chicks. But remember, birds are designed to fly. They have hollow bones and feather shafts which allows them to be fairly large and sturdy without being heavy. Even the largest Great Blue Heron only weighs 6 to 8 pounds.

About three weeks after being laid the chicks hatch, but are quite small and weak with closed eyes and no feathers. The parents simply regurgitate food into the nest so that the chicks can eat.

Perhaps not the cutest babies you have seen, but comically attractive in their own way. It took one week for the chicks to develop the three colors in their new feathers and to be strong enough to take food from a parent's mouth.

True of all of the heron species, efficient hunting – using a beak designed for grasping live prey – and superb vision are two reasons they've been able to come back from near extinction.

In the warmer months Tricolored Herons populate the entire Eastern coastline as well as the Gulf Coast where they may be known as Louisiana Herons.

In just one more week of eating high protein fresh fish the chicks become much larger. They will soon start to explore the nest area on foot, but are generally still and quiet to avoid being detected by predators. However, when a parent approaches with food all rules are broken and the chicks will squawk loudly to make sure the parent knows it is feeding time.

As mid-summer approaches the Tricolored Heron chicks have fledged, begun to hunt on their own, and are ready to start their lives in the Lowcountry marshes. But, the juveniles may still remain close to the rookery where their parents built the nest in hopes that they may get one last delivered meal.

A rookery full of the various herons is one of the natural attractions that all should find and appreciate. The Lowcountry has numerous public viewing sites that make spring in the south an extra special treat.

EGRETTA TRICOLOR

It will be some time before the juvenile Tricolored Heron develops the plumage of the adult, but both the young and mature coloration present a very attractive appearance.

Great Blue Herons, Little Blue Herons and Tricolored Herons are the heron species you will most likely see in the Lowcountry, but there are others you should be on the lookout for as well.

Green Heron
Butorides virescens

AN EVEN SMALLER heron found hunting in the Lowcountry lagoon waters is the Green Heron, which stands 18 inches tall. Because of its smaller size, and the fact that it's not as plentiful as some of the other species, the Green Heron is not as easy to see in nature. Like the Tricolored Heron, the Green Heron is named for its distinctive and beautiful green feathers displayed along its back.

As you may have surmised, it is classified as a heron because of its long neck, which it uses to catch prey while walking along

The captured worm will probably be a quick snack, but it may be used as bait to attract much bigger prey.

BUTORIDES VIRESCENS

the marsh or lagoon shoreline. The very large feet seen in all herons allow them to traverse soggy and muddy areas without sinking in. With large feet and light bodies, some species—like this one—can even walk on floating vegetation with no difficulty. For this reason, the Green Heron may appear much taller than its 18 inches at first glance.

Many of the Lowcountry marsh birds nest in large shared colonies called rookeries. The Green Heron prefers to be more solitary when choosing a nesting site. It builds its nest in a tree overhanging the lagoon water, but away from colonies of other nesting birds. Three to five chicks share the nest and hatch in about 23 days. After hatching in late April or early May, the chicks are able to move about in the tree branches by late May. By using their feet and rudimentary wings for balance they are able to move quite deftly through the branches.

Once the true flight feathers develop, the juvenile Green Herons will begin hunting along the lagoon shoreline, occasionally using a technique unlike any other of the marsh and lagoon birds. Green Herons have been observed actually fishing with bait. They will drop insects, or other food items, into the water and wait for a fish to be attracted to the bait. When a fish ventures out of hiding to eat the bait, it becomes the heron's meal—a very interesting adaptation, for sure.

Here you can see the Green Heron's head and neck retracted. Previously it displayed its full 18 inch height as well as an intermediate position. Indeed, quite variable as the situation merits.

Normally well hidden in the lagoon side nesting area, the young Green Herons will venture out of hiding as they get closer to fledging time, when they will be able to fly to the lagoon shore to feed for the first time.

As you've seen, some marsh and lagoon bird juveniles have a very different feather pattern than the adults have. Here is another example. Compare this young heron perched in the rookery to the adult Black-crowned Night Heron.

Black-crowned Night Heron
Nycticorax nycticorax

As mentioned earlier, the various birds that share the Lowcountry marsh and lagoon waters as their habitat have a slightly different niche when it comes to eating. Some hunt for food in the deep water, others stay in the shallower areas and some fish from the shore. As its name implies, the Black-crowned Night Heron has filled an entirely different niche. It does its hunting at night to lessen competition from other species. With large eyes and reflective retinas, it can see prey by starlight or moonlight.

Black-crowned Night Herons roost during the day and then exhibit their nearly four foot wing span as they fly off to their favorite hunting ground as the sun begins to set.

As sunset approaches, the Black-crowned Night Heron spreads its 44-inch wings and heads for a nearby marsh to eat. A distinguishing characteristic is the short distance the legs extend behind the tail feathers in flight.
Right: A young Black-crowned Heron is obtaining its adult plumage at about three years of age.

Earlier, I explained how many species go through quite a transformation in plumage as they mature from juvenile to adult. Black-crowned Night Herons also show a fairly drastic change in plumage as they transition from the juvenile stage into the adult breeding stage. The young demonstrate a much more uniform coloration, with predominantly buff or grey feathers speckled with patterned white areas. As they approach the adult breeding phase, which takes about three years, their identification as Black-crowned Night Herons becomes much more apparent.

The Black-crowned Heron is indeed very attractive in either juvenile or adult plumage. Theirs eyes are designed to gather enough light to see potential prey in dim, nighttime light.

The marsh and lagoon herons found in the Lowcountry make up a diverse group comprised of six species. Each one has its own unique and interesting characteristics which make observing the herons a most enjoyable experience.

Interestingly, the Black-crowned Night Heron attains its breeding season plumage as early as December for the next year's mating season. Their black crowns produce long white plumes, which drape down the back of their necks. After the male establishes a territory in the rookery, he will bend, bow and stretch to show the female his white plumes. Once together, the pair will construct a nest and share in the incubation and rearing of their three to five hatchlings.

Six or seven weeks after hatching, Black-crowned Night Heron chicks may be seen perfecting their hunting skills at the borders of their rookery lagoon. Soon, the juveniles will scatter to establish their own territories and gradually mature into adults.

It is a treat if you can observe awake and alert Black-crowned Night Herons in the daytime. White feathers extending down the back of the neck start to develop as the breeding season approaches.

NYCTICORAX NYCTICORAX

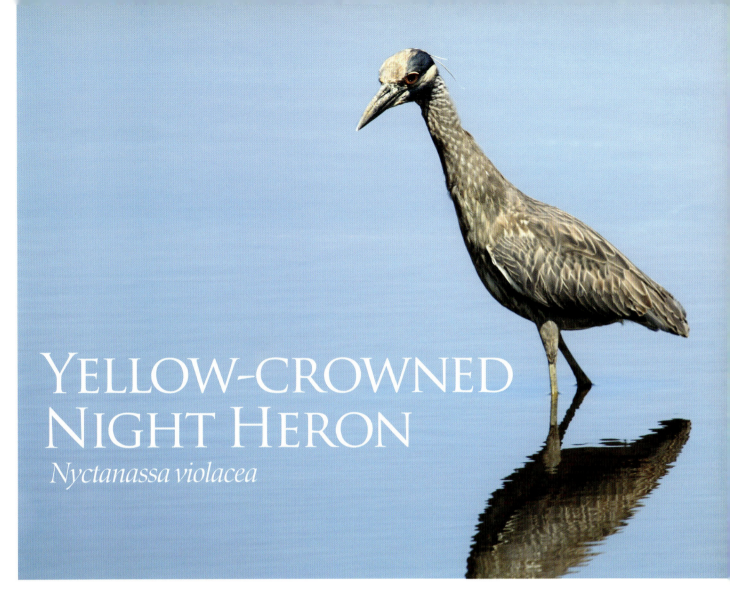

Yellow-crowned Night Heron
Nyctanassa violacea

You know that the night herons hunt mainly after dusk, but, on occasion, the Yellow-crowned Night Herons can be seen searching for food during daylight hours as well.

Also nocturnal, but not exclusively, is the Yellow-crowned Night Heron. These 24-inch birds show a distinctive, beautiful feather pattern, punctuated by a crown of yellow feathers on the top of their heads, which becomes even more distinctive during the mating season. They may not be seen in colonies occupied by many different species as often as some of the other Lowcountry marsh and lagoon birds, but can be seen roosting during the day time, either in a rookery or in their own more private resting habitats. Like the Black-crowned Heron, the Yellow-crowned Heron also exhibits long plumes cascading down from the back of its head during the mate attracting phase of its mating season.

The Yellow-crowned young look nearly identical to the Black-crowned young, but smaller light spots and a thicker, darker, beak make distinguishing the two possible. Below right: The mature Yellow-crowned Night Heron in full mating plumage.

Both males and females look identical, but, once again, the juveniles look like an entirely different species. In fact, as you probably have noted, they look very similar to the Black-crowned Night Heron young. The Yellow-crowned Night Heron immature birds have a slightly thicker and darker beak and the white pattern on their grayish-brown feathers is made up of smaller spots than those seen on the Black-crowned young.

Whether feeding at night or during the day, the Yellow-crowned Night Heron has a varied diet consisting of nearly anything it can catch and consume. As with many of the marsh and lagoon birds, the varied diet helps assure its survival if one food source becomes scarce for any reason.

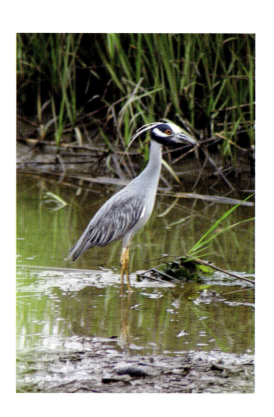

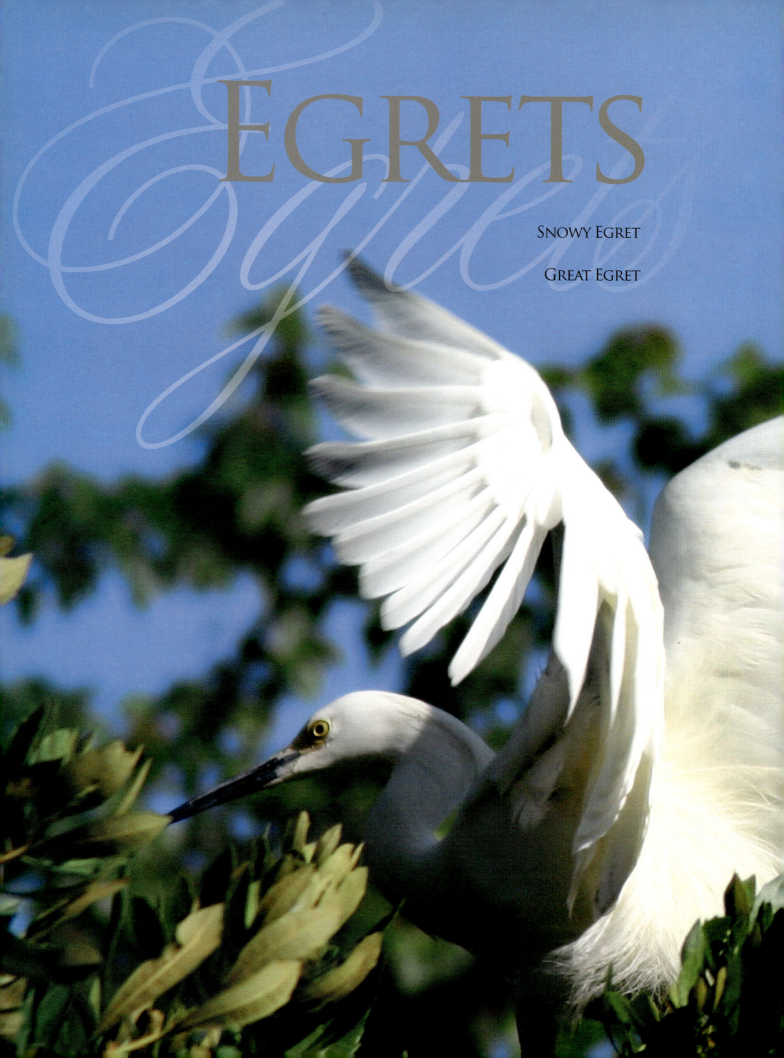
EGRETS

Snowy Egret

Great Egret

Snowy Egret
Egretta thula

Bird classification can be confusing. Egrets are herons, but are commonly called egrets due to their white color. However, the Tricolored Heron, not white, is grouped with the egrets even though it is a heron. See? Confusing. Early classification attempts placed various birds together if they shared similar body shapes and habits. Now, with the advent of genetic testing, true relationships will be established and classification will, undoubtedly, be quite different in the years ahead. For now, we have to use the many current resources to understand bird taxonomy, and even these do not always agree. The two egrets that occupy the Lowcountry marsh and lagoon waters were so named because of the French term *aigrette*, which refers to the brush-like plumes seen in birds during their courtship and breeding cycles. Because the plumes of the white herons are so beautiful, and were once very popular with hat designers, as mentioned earlier, the term *aigrette* became permanently linked to these stunning white birds.

The Snowy Egret is the smaller of our two marsh egrets at about two feet in height. The beautiful brush-like plumes, which gave the egrets their name, are exhibited during the spring mating season. The Snowy Egret will share its nesting with other marsh and lagoon bird species in large rookery colonies. The male will perform his mate-attracting ritual repeatedly and loudly, then, once he has found a partner, he, like most of the birds in the rookery, will share in the care and feeding of the chicks.

Egrets are so named because of the French term *aigrette*, which refers to the brush-like plumes they exhibit during courtship.

The throwing back of the head accompanied by loud vocalization is performed a few times in succession as part of the mating ritual.

Chicks have an "egg tooth," a hard projection on the tip of their beak, which aids in pipping, the process of breaking out of the shell. Pipping can still be an exhausting task, however. Right: Upon becoming a new parent, the Snowy Egret's role is to catch small fish and then regurgitate them so that the chicks can eat.

While one parent is attending to the eggs, or later, the chicks, the other will be at the edge of the water running quickly to catch any food source it has spotted. If the eggs have hatched it will be gathering food which it will take back to the nest for regurgitating directly into the hungry chicks' mouths. Interestingly, when one parent returns to the nest to relieve the other, it must perform a display ritual to be recognized. Otherwise, it may be perceived as an intruder and chased away.

The larger rookery birds must construct their nests toward the end of the tree branches so that they can more easily maneuver around the nest. The Snowy Egret, being quite small, can place nests toward the center of the tree, which may offer better protection from storms and predators.

The chicks, as with other birds, have an egg tooth at the tip of their beak which aids them in breaking out of their shell. Soon, the egg tooth will disappear and the young Snowy Egret's pink bill will be evident. It too will change over time and may even be yellow for a while before becoming the black beak seen in the adults.

The young will explore the branches on foot for about one

month prior to fledging and developing their flight feathers on their wings, which will eventually grow to about three feet from tip to tip.

At least there is no confusion in this species about the juvenile being a Snowy Egret. Except for being a bit smaller than an adult, the maturing birds look very similar to what they will look like when they reach full maturity. Some of the young will remain in the vicinity of the rookery for a few weeks more before leaving to establish their independent lifestyle in one of the Lowcountry's numerous marshes.

You may think his right foot is wet up to the ankle, but that is not the case. Look at the left leg—the yellow 'foot' is really just the toes. The foot bones are fused and extend all the way to the bend just below the white feathers you see at their lowest point. The bend is actually the bird's heel and ankle. The knee is hidden by feathers and is up close to the bird's body.

The joy of observing the Lowcountry's marsh and lagoon birds is greatly enhanced by the myriad of colors and patterns the water takes on as the sun, wind and reflections create new, beautiful views with each passing moment.

EGRETTA THULA

The Snowy Egret may be small in stature, and may lack the flashy plumage of some other birds, but they are certainly unrivaled in their appealing appearance.

Great Egret
Ardea alba

Perhaps the most visible Lowcountry marsh and lagoon bird—because of its large size, 39 inches, and its brilliant white color—is the Great Egret. These egrets spend more time here than some of the other marsh and lagoon birds, so are relatively easy to see and enjoy.

I don't have to remind you that the long showy feathers mean that it's mating season, but I will mention again that the lores, the area of skin in front of the eyes, also change to a brilliant green and are an important part of the bird's total alteration used to attract a mate each spring.

Once the pair has bonded and constructed a nest in the rookery, it is time for them to start a new generation of Great Egrets.

The spring plumage, the color change in the lores, and the mutual displays eventually lead to the mating act itself. As with most birds, mating occurs while the male maintains his balance while standing on the female's back. Once the egg is fertilized, it will descend through the female's single oviduct, a common feature in birds. While descending, the shell will form around the embryo with its yolk and albumen food sup-

It will be some time before these two Great Egrets reach adulthood, but when they do their hormones will trigger instinctive behavior and they, too, will begin a spring ritual designed to ensure that they will pass on their genes to the next generation.

ply, needed for the approximately three week development seen in the majority of bird species. The egg, and soon possibly as many as five more, will be deposited in the three foot nest.

The Great Egret's oldest eggs will hatch the earliest, and the chicks will be slightly more mature and stronger than their younger siblings that hatch a few days later. If the parents are extremely efficient, and if there is an abundant food supply, there may be no sibling rivalry. But, this is not usually the case; most of the time, the older chicks will actually expel the younger and weaker chicks from the nest. The parents do not intervene in this seemingly (to us) cruel behavior, because it is simply nature's way of insuring

When the chicks are young, a parent may be able to provide enough food for all of the hungry mouths. But, as the demand for more food increases as the young get larger, it's possible that only the strongest and most aggressive will receive adequate nutrition. It seems unfair to our way of thinking, but, often, that is the way nature works.

The early spring dormant grasses serve to highlight the exquisite feathers of the Great Egrets displaying their mating season plumage. Here, the contrast between the all white Egret and the dark plumed Anhinga provide a sample of the variety you can observe in the Lowcountry birds.

that some birds will survive to carry on the species' genes to future generations, thus guaranteeing the survival of the species. That is how life in the natural world has been for millions of years.

We can all hope that our future generations will be able to witness the flight and beauty of the Great Egret as we do today.

Ardea Alba

White Ibis

Glossy Ibis

White Ibis
Eudocimus albus

Ubiquitous in most areas of the Lowcountry, this marsh and lagoon bird has learned that hunting for grubs, worms and bugs can be easier in the open fairways of the numerous golf courses than digging in the marsh mud for a meal. Often seen in flocks composed of just a few birds, they may also form groups composed of dozens. You may see them fly in 'V' formation from feeding ground to feeding ground. Once on dry land, or in the marsh waters, they quickly scurry about digging for food with their long curved beaks.

The White Ibis demonstrates the advantage of having juveniles that do not have the all white coloration of the adults. The mottled brown and white of the younger Ibis makes it easier to blend in with the dormant grasses in and around the marsh in the early spring.

The young White Ibis probes the mud at the bottom of a lagoon, searching for small animals, while the Snowy Egret waits for fish that may move out of their hiding places when disturbed by the ibis.

Being camouflaged, rather than all white, certainly is an advantage when being hunted by predators that feed on young birds.

By adulthood, the White Ibis is indeed white. Black wing tips show in flight, but not when the bird is on the ground searching for a meal.

The Ibis share the reproductive scenario displayed by most of the other birds I've shown. The male attracts his mate by pointing his curved beak skyward as well as by showing off by using it to preen himself. The pair will join many other Ibis and construct their nest in a rookery. They will raise two to five chicks, which will leave the nest in about six weeks. In time, they will mature into 25-inch adults with a wingspan of about three feet.

The young White Ibis display beaks superbly adapted for probing deep into mud and turf. Even their eye color will change as they transition from the camouflage plumage to the all white color of adulthood.

Not seen in the White Ibis while feeding, the back wing tips visible in flight add to the attractiveness of this remarkable species.

Maturing juveniles will join the adults and form flocks made up of 20 or more individuals flying in a 'V' formation as they migrate to the north when the temperature increases in the Lowcountry.

Glossy Ibis
Plegadis falcinellus

Perhaps the most attractively plumed wading bird, the Glossy Ibis migrated from Africa relatively recently and now can be seen along the eastern and gulf coast during different times of the year. They winter in the Lowcountry and along the Gulf of Mexico shoreline.

The Glossy Ibis is just slightly smaller than the White Ibis. And, as you surmised from its name and curved beak, it shares similar hunting techniques. It probes the mud in search of crabs, insects and even small reptiles and amphibians.

The density of melanin gives us our multitude of skin colors and also produces some of the color in bird feathers. Brighter colors come from carotenoids and the refraction of sunlight as it strikes the bird's feathers. Of all the Lowcountry's marsh and lagoon birds, there may been none more striking than the Glossy Ibis.

Like the other marsh and lagoon birds, the Glossy Ibis displays its feathers, beautiful and iridescent, in the early spring as a sign to potential mates that it is mature and ready to participate in this year's mating activities.

A couple produce three or four chicks in twig nests located in trees lining the Lowcountry waters and share the nesting site with the colonies of White Ibis, herons and egrets. As with the other species, the Glossy Ibis parents share the responsibility of incubating, but the female does the majority of the work.

The Glossy Ibis population is not nearly as large as that of the White Ibis, which makes seeing them in the wild more difficult, but, as you can see, well worth the effort.

Glossy Ibis that inhabit northern portions of the East Coast spend the winter in the Lowcountry. I hope you have the chance to see one in its natural habitat.

A rainbow of colors, and even added iridescence during the mating season, make it easy to understand how the Glossy Ibis got its common name.

RAILS

King Rail

Clapper Rail

American Coot

Common Moorhen

King Rail
Rallus elegans

The King Rail is one of the more secretive birds found in the Lowcountry marshes. Because it much prefers walking to flying, and because it does its foraging in the tall, dense grass at the margins of the marsh, it is usually fairly difficult to see. At extreme high tide, it may be forced out of the protective cover of the marsh vegetation by the rising water.

The King Rail is about 15 inches in length and possesses feathers often referred to as cinnamon colored. It will eat both plant seeds and fruits, along with any available small animals, such as fish, frogs and crabs. The King Rail, like the owl, regurgitates indigestible food in the form of a pellet, a behavior not observed in many other marsh birds.

The King Rail male courts the female by offering her a crab. When she accepts the offer, they build a ground level nest in the marsh grass and may hide it by arching grass over the nest. She produces a fairly large clutch of about ten eggs, which both parents incubate. Young King Rail chicks spend very little time in the nest and work on their hunting skills in the marsh grass while waiting two months for their flight feathers to develop.

If you are a fan of dinosaurs, you know that current opinion has it that today's birds are descendants of the ancient dinosaurs. Interestingly, the King Rail chicks, while still very young, have a vestigial claw as part of their wing bones.

As they're usually well hidden in the tall, dense grass at the edge of a marsh, it is indeed a treat to observe the King Rail making a rare appearance in the open.

Clapper Rail
Rallus longirostris

When the gravitational pull of the sun and moon work together, at the new moon and full moon, the tides in the marshes can be quite a bit higher than the average tide. At these times, another very secretive rail may be seen as it becomes necessary for it to leave the protection of the marsh grasses to avoid the rising water. The Clapper Rail looks very similar to the King Rail, but it is smaller and has feathers that have a more gray appearance than those on the King Rail's cinnamon colored feathers.

Some sources classify the two as variations of the same species because they have been known to interbreed and produce chicks.

Clapper Rails rarely fly and usually remain in the dense grass, which they can navigate easily while hunting for invertebrates because they can make themselves narrow enough to squeeze through the clumps of vegetation when necessary.

Clapper Rails are more easily heard than seen, and a breeding pair will strengthen their mutual bond by coordinating their calls until it sounds as if only one bird is chattering.

The Clapper Rail is said to be 14½ inches in size, but that is its length from the tip of its beak to the end of the tail feathers. In height, while walking out of the flooded marsh at high tide, it may not be much larger than it is pictured here. Small, secretive and most appealing.

American Coot
Fulica americana

AMERICAN COOTS are also placed in the rail family, but have a very different appearance and behavior than that of the King Rail and Clapper Rail. The American Coot can easily be seen in the Lowcountry lagoons as they swim in groups while feeding on both plants and animals. They are distinguished by the front shield on their beaks, which develops between the eyes and becomes red in the adults during the spring mating season.

They will swim away from a disturbance most of the year, but are protective of their nests when eggs or chicks are present and will attempt to chase away predators. This behavior may continue even after the chicks become independent and, of-

The American Coot has unusual lobes on its feet that aid in swimming—and "walking" on water!

ten, this leads to the adults being captured by hunting animals, or even other birds, such as hawks and eagles.

Immature American Coots have a paler color and lack the shield portion of the upper beak. When they grow to adulthood they will be about 16 inches in overall length.

When seen swimming, the American Coot may appear more closely related to the ducks than the rails, but ducks have true webbed feet while the American Coot possesses special structures on its toes called lobes. The lobes are flaps of flesh that fold back when the foot moves forward and extend to the side as the foot paddles to the rear. This provides for an efficient way of swimming through the lagoon water.

Larger birds need to produce forward motion so that their wings can produce enough lift to initiate flying. Some birds leap from perches, some run on land, and water birds skitter across the water using their feet to assist them in gaining the needed forward speed.

The American Coot shows you its lobed feet and also demonstrates how to stay warm on a cool winter day.

You have tiny muscles attached to your body hairs. When these **erector pili** muscles make your hair stand up, the hairs pull on your skin and produce 'goose bumps' or 'chill bumps'. Birds have similar **pennati** muscles to fluff up their feathers and produce air pockets for insulation; quite a different look for the same bird.

Common Moorhen
Gallinula chloropus

During the bird's mating season the Common Moorhen may be unmistakable because of the large, very red, frontal shield that makes up the majority of its beak. As with special plumage seen in other birds, the bright red beak shield developed as a means of attracting the opposite sex during the breeding cycle. After the chicks have hatched and the adult's hormones diminish, the red beak gradually fades. Immature Common Moorhens also lack the beak shield which they will eventually develop as they reach full maturity.

The Common Moorhen is only about one foot long, and its wings are only 21 to 23 inches long—short and stubby compared to the long wings seen in the graceful Herons and Egrets. But, with rapid wing beats they can fly efficiently for long distances when migrating.

The Common Moorhen is also known as the Common Gallinule. The distinctive red beak shield is not seen in juvenile birds and fades as the breeding season wanes.

The genus name of the Common Moorhen, Gallinula, means chicken like. When you have the opportunity to see them swimming, you will see that they bob their heads forward and back like a chicken does when walking.

The Common Moorhen lacks webbed feet and lobed toes, but still swims easily. Its large feet, as you've learned, allows it to walk on muddy bottoms as well as on top of floating vegetation, its main source of nutrition. However, it also eats a wide variety of other plants and small animals. It may even be seen walking on the shore pecking at seeds—again, resembling a chicken.

The Common Moorhen nesting pair, which are nearly identical, carry out an interesting activity. After the slightly larger male attracts a female with gifts of plants and a display of his tail feathers, they will proceed to build several nests on the shore and quite near to the water. In one nest, the female will lay one off white, speckled egg per day for up to as many as twelve days. When the chicks hatch, in about 20 days, they are very soon self-sufficient, or precocial, but unable to fly for another six weeks or so. The original nest could get very crowded, so the chicks spend their nights in one of those many other nests the parents constructed just for that purpose; interesting. If the weather conditions allow it, the pair may use the same nests again for a second brood of chicks.

Feather 'fluffing' to produce air pockets for added insulation may be necessary on cold winter days – even here in the Lowcountry.

The Wilson's Snipe is 10 inches long overall. If you subtract the length of its proportionally very long beak, you can see that it is, in fact, quite a small marsh species.

Wilson's Snipe
Gallinago delicata

Here's a great example of how difficult it is to classify birds: Some noted ornithologists say that the Common Snipe is indeed common, while others claim that it's extremely rare in America and that it is the Wilson's Snipe that we may see in the Lowcountry marshes. Because the two are nearly identical it is difficult for the casual observer to tell the difference, and a close examination of the tail feathers may be necessary to distinguish the two. The more current opinion is that we are observing the Wilson's Snipe in this part of the country.

The Wilson's Snipe is noted for its very long beak in comparison to its body size. The bird is about 10 inches long overall, but that measurement includes the long straight beak it uses to probe the mud for a meal at the marsh and lagoon margins.

The snipe's procedure for attracting a mate is quite different from other techniques you've been reading about. The male Wilson's Snipe performs his mating ritual not only from a perch, but also from the air. A loud vocal call while perched is part of its complex ritual. Then—and you haven't read of a technique like this before—the bird flies rapidly and dives to increase speed until the air rushing through its tail feathers causes them to vibrate and produce a series of humming sounds somewhat similar to an Owl's hoots; these sounds are designed to attract the attention of nearby females.

The Wilson's Snipe, as well as the rails, is quite secretive and usually remains out of sight in the vegetation. When it is startled, the snipe will fly in an erratic pattern, attempting to outmaneuver predators. There was a time, in the Lowcountry and elsewhere, when the majority of the population had to grow their own fruit and vegetables, raise livestock and hunt and fish for additional food. Even though very small, quick and elusive, the snipe, as well as many other birds, were hunted for food. Only the best hunters were able to shoot the quick and elusive snipe, and the best of these marksmen became known as snipers. Even though it may have different connotations, depending on who is doing the shooting, you still hear the term sniper used today.

The Wilson's Snipe's long bill, while highly unusual serves it well in the collection of food.

The Wilson's Snipe's color pattern is designed to help it blend in with the reeds and grasses so predators will have difficulty seeing it.

You can also see the long pointed beak in action as it probes deep into the soil to extract the small creatures that live there.

Killdeer
Charadrius vociferous

You can distinguish the Killdeer from its close relatives by observing the double ringed feather pattern around its neck and upper breast.

The killdeer is a master of both diversification and deception. Earlier I wrote that birds which get their nutrition from the Lowcountry marsh and lagoon waters would be the ones pictured here. Killdeer are technically Plovers, shorebirds seen at the coast, but they have adapted to many different environments. They can be found in a wide range of areas where gravel covers the ground. It may be at the shore or far from water in meadows, roadsides or even on the tar and gravel rooftops of city buildings. However, a significant number of Killdeer also inhabit the mudflats and shorelines of the Lowcountry's marshes and lagoons, so they do qualify as marsh and lagoon birds even though these areas may not be the species' exclusive niche.

The male and female look very similar, and there is no drastic change in appearance from the chick to the adult Killdeer, as in some other birds. The male's courtship routine consists of using its vociferous call while flying and showing off his deceptive abilities while on the ground. It is the loud, frequent call—sounding like "kill deer"—which gives the bird both its common and scientific names.

The Killdeer is a master of deception. It does not nest high in a tree, or hide its nest in the grasses, but rather, it simply lays its eggs in a shallow depression, in an area covered by small stones and gravel.

The female deposits the well-camouflaged speckled eggs in gravel that closely resembles them. Egg-laying may take a

period of a few days to complete, so neither parent sits on the nest until all eggs have been laid. Then, when a parent sits on the nest, its warmth initiates the incubation of all of the eggs at the same time. The eggs are relatively large for a 10-inch bird because they contain more yolk and albumen than other eggs from comparable sized birds. This is because the Killdeer chicks are precocial. They incubate longer than average, and the extra food in the egg allows the chicks to be more mature and hatch ready to fend for themselves. Within a short time after hatching, the chicks can run about hunting for their own food.

Because the Killdeer nests are out in the open, protected only by their blending in with the surrounding stones, the Killdeer has developed a unique means of protecting the eggs from predators. If a parent perceives a threat, it will leave the nest and put on an effective charade. It will act like it has a broken wing—holding the wing in an unusual position and walking away from the nest with a tilted, 'injured' body—while pretending it's trying to fly. A hungry predator will think it may have an easy time capturing the adult Killdeer. When the Killdare parent has lured the hunter far enough from the nest, it will suddenly have a miraculous recovery and fly away. Very clever.

As the tide ebbs in a Lowcountry marsh, the mud, teeming with a variety of small creatures, is exposed and allows the Killdeer to probe for its food – getting a bit of a dirty face, but still finely feathered.

The marsh and lagoon shore is just one of the many habitats the Killdeer has adapted to. The more areas a species can survive in the better its chance of survival if conditions become unfavorable in one of these areas.

Spotted Sandpiper
Actitis macularius

When you see the name Sandpiper, you probably think of the ocean shore and the little birds that run with very rapid leg movements to search for food in the wet sand as each breaking wave recedes. Sandpipers, as well as Piping Plovers, get their name from their vocalizations. There are about three dozen species of sandpipers and many of them are found at the shore. The Spotted Sandpiper, however, while it may sometimes be found at the shore, is one sandpiper whose normal habitat is in the marshes, lagoons or ponds. It has the largest breeding range of any of the sandpipers, and it can be found nesting throughout the northern portion of the United States and into Canada. The Spotted Sandpiper may be seen in the Lowcountry during the winter months, or in the spring, as it passes through on its migration to the north from as far away as South America.

The Spotted Sandpiper, which is larger than some sandpipers seen at the shore at about 7 inches in length, has two very distinct and unusual characteristics that will help you identify it even from a distance. The first is its flight; they fly with very stiff wings that move up and down a very short distance, but rapidly, to create lift and forward flight. The second distinguishing characteristic is its teetering. Spotted Sandpipers almost constantly raise and lower their rump area in less than one-second intervals. The purpose of this repetitive movement is not known, and it begins in less than one hour after the Spotted Sandpipers hatch from their egg; an unusual behavior, but one that is very interesting to witness.

Many of the birds I've shown share in all parental duties, while other birds leave the incubation up to the female, the male ceasing his duties as soon as the eggs are deposited in a nest. Once again, the Spotted Sandpiper is somewhat unique; the female arrives at the nesting site first and it is her job to claim a territory. Then, she will mate with more than one male and each male will then take on the role of incubating the eggs and protecting the new chicks. The female can store sperm from one male for nearly a month and then lay fertilized eggs that another male will incubate in a separate nest. The female may be the mother of anywhere from a dozen to 20 chicks being incubated by males in four different nests which are located on the ground near a marsh, pond or lake. The female will assist and incubate eggs and care for chicks if there are not enough males available to care for all of the nests.

You may see one of these very handsome Spotted Sandpipers walking along the water's edge in search of small insects or other invertebrates.

Wood Stork
Mycteria americana

The Great Egret has to see its prey in order to capture it, but the Wood Stork relies on the very sensitive nerves within its beak to detect potential food, so being able to see into the water is not necessary.

The birds you have seen so far are classified in groups with similar traits or behaviors and may be closely related to other members within that group. However, the Wood Stork is unique. It has no relatives in the Lowcountry. In fact, it is the only stork in North America. Its distinguishing characteristic, which makes it unique, is the fact that, unlike other birds, it lacks a syrinx, or voice box. To make a sound, chiefly to attract a mate, it quickly snaps its beak shut. Because of the large size and structure of the beak, a considerable noise can be generated.

It is not the lack of a syrinx that gives this bird its name, however, but rather its posture while standing. Stork comes from

an Old English term meaning "stiff."

Wood Storks were killed for their feathers during the fashion trend described previously, but are now even more threatened because of the destruction of their natural habitat, the wetlands. Their population was documented to have risen from near extinction to nearly 60,000 at one point, but there are much fewer now because of human activity. Recent counts have shown some improvement, but care must be exercised so that continued development does not cause their population to drop further.

The Wood Stork is, perhaps, the closest thing we have to a true Lowcountry bird because it only breeds in the Carolinas, Georgia and portions of Florida.

There are at least two ways to measure bird size: height and weight. The Great Blue Heron may be the tallest, but the Wood Stork is the heaviest bird seen regularly in the Lowcountry marshes; it can weigh over seven pounds, with some reaching as much as ten pounds.

As mentioned, the beak is used to create sound as a mating ritual, but it has also adapted to being extremely efficient for capturing food. The Wood Stork does not rely on seeing its prey, as is the case with many marsh and lagoon hunters. Instead, it uses its beak, lined with millions of sensitive nerves that allow it to capture food while sweeping the beak back and forth

When visibility is possible the Wood Stork will use its wings to create shade so that water reflections do not hinder its ability to use its eyes to assist in the search for food.

in the water and mud at the bottom of the marsh. There are people who study such things, and it has been reported that the Wood Stork can close its mouth extremely fast to capture a morsel of food—not in a few thousandths of a second, but in a few millionths of a second; perhaps the fastest reflex seen in vertebrate animals. They seem to prefer narrower bodies of water to carry out their search for food, and they even delay their mating activity until later in the spring so that the water pools have shrunk to the point that the fish become concentrated and easier to capture.

Beautiful in flight, Wood Storks may ride air currents thousands of feet above the ground. They have even been observed doing rolls at high altitude. In fact, the first attempts at flight by humans used Wood Stork wings as the model for the first glider and aircraft wings.

As it matures, the feathered neck of the Wood Stork loses its plumage and the wrinkled skin of the adult bird indicates that it is mature and ready to find a mate. Once paired, the Wood Stork couple will often mate for life. The female will lay three

to five tennis ball sized eggs in their nest, located, often with many other Wood Stork pairs, in a tree growing out of the marsh. Both parents will share the chick's incubation followed by their feeding. The chicks demand fifteen feedings a day for a period of nine weeks. Yes, those that studied Wood Stork feeding have figured it takes about four hundred pounds of fish to raise the chicks in one nest and keep the parents nourished as well.

The reason Wood Storks build their nests—and whole colonies—in a wet area is an excellent example of the complicated relationships nature supports. When

Below you see the neck feathers that let you know that this is a young Wood Stork. Above, in a mature Wood Stork, the feathers have disappeared and the wrinkled skin is evident.

there is sufficient water at the base of the tree, raccoons—always on the lookout for Wood Stork eggs—are often taken by hungry alligators for a meal. If the area is dry, there are no alligators to control the raccoon population, hence the raccoons can severely deplete the number of Wood Stork eggs in the colony. As humans alter the environment, we must be aware of these complex interactions in nature and how we may be affecting them. A great number of species may be adversely affected by the actions we take if these actions alter the ecology of the Lowcountry, even in a seemingly minor way.

Wood Storks nest in large colonies along with herons, egrets and ibis. However, they may begin their nest construction in these rookeries after the other species eggs have already hatched and the chicks are growing.

Double-crested Cormorant
Phalacrocorax auritus

You have seen a number of Lowcountry marsh birds that hunt for food while walking—either wading in the water or walking through the grass at the edge of the marsh or lagoon. Some use their beaks to capture prey from the water while others probe the mud in search of nutrients. Some hunt during the day and the Night-Herons are more active after sundown. Well, as I stated earlier, the variety of hunting techniques lessens direct competition for food. And yes, there is an entirely different method of hunting used by a bird you are undoubtedly familiar with, the Double-crested Cormorant. The Cormorants dive beneath the surface and, using their webbed feet, actually

The early bird catches the fish. The Double-crested Cormorant lands at sunrise to begin its search for fish beneath the lagoon water. Its hooked beak helps hold the fish securely until it can be ingested.

swim underwater to hunt for fish. They then use their hooked beaks to capture their prey.

Cormorants have glands known as preen glands, which are found near the base of the tail feathers in birds; but they do not distribute the protective, water resistant oil to their outer feathers. Therefore, their feathers are able to absorb water, making the Cormorants heavier and less buoyant; this allows them to dive and remain submerged for easier fishing.

Cormorants are another of the more easy to spot species; they are large, at 32 inches, and great numbers of them can be seen standing on the shore with their 48 to 50 inch wings spread out to dry. They are not in the Lowcountry for the entire

Rows of feathers on either side of the head and located a little above and behind the eyes are visible during mating season and give the Double-crested Cormorant its name.

Because Cormorants have little oil to protect their feathers from water absorption, they dry them between their diving excursions.

year; they move farther north during the warming trend in the spring.

In the air, Cormorants move quite swiftly and, while landing, descend rapidly, using both their wings and their webbed feet to quickly decelerate before touching down in the water.

Young Cormorants display lighter feathers, especially on the breast area. As they mature, they will become darker all over and, during mating season, will display two rows of feathers on either side of the

As the immature, tan colored Cormorant ages, it will develop the dark color seen in the adult.

top of their head; thus their name, Double-crested. The male's crest feathers become more prominent than those of the female. Adult pairs will mate and raise one brood of chicks each spring. Nesting in colonies, the Cormorant will construct a nest out of sticks and nearly anything else lying around that could be used for nest building. Like the Herons and Egrets, the Cormorant parents regurgitate fish to feed the young chicks.

Cormorants have been know to live into their teens, but about a six year life span is more typical.

The Cormorant's skill at fishing has been taken advantage of in some cultures. People tie a cord around the base of the Cormorant's neck, which allows the bird to eat small fish, but prevents it from swallowing large fish. When a large fish is captured, the bird is pulled to its handler who takes the fish from the Cormorant's throat for use by family members or to sell at the local market.

There is an old expression: "Your eyes are bigger than your stomach." Meaning: We sometimes take more food than we can eat simply because it looks so good. The Cormorant above tried to swallow the large fish for a long time before finally giving up.

ANHINGA
Anhinga anhinga

FROM A DISTANCE you may think you are seeing a Cormorant with its wings spread out to dry, but upon closer inspection you'll realize that you do not see the hooked beak of the Cormorant, but rather a sharp pointed beak. This bird, with the pointed beak, is the Anhinga, and it has a very similar niche, or environmental role, to that of the Cormorant. Like the Cormorant, it hunts by diving and swimming underwater to capture fish, but it uses a slightly different technique. The Anhinga uses its sharp pointed beak to stab the fish it is hunting. In fact, one of its common names is the Black

This male Anhinga with its black neck held out of the water shows how it got the nickname Snake Bird. It is also known as the Black Darter because of the way it uses that pointed beak to spear fish.

Darter because of the way it sticks its beak into the fish to secure them while returning to the surface to eat, yet another example of nature's diversity and why observing it can be so enjoyable and so fascinating. Other common names for the Anhinga include Water Turkey and Snake Bird: Water Turkey, because of the way it fans out its long tail feathers to dry; and Snake Bird, because when it's partially submerged, only its long neck and head are visible, making it resemble a snake about to strike. Its common and scientific name, Anhinga, comes from the Tupi language indigenous to what is now Brazil; it means Devil Bird.

The Anhinga is one of the larger marsh and lagoon birds at 35 inches in overall length. When its wings are spread to the side to dry, they extend about 45 inches from tip to tip. Anhingas lack the Preen, or oil, glands so they cannot coat their feathers to make them more water resistant. This helps in their ability to dive beneath the water easily, but requires that they spend a considerable amount of time drying their feathers so they can fly if necessary and also to help maintain a comfortable temperature.

Anhingas will stay in the Lowcountry to nest in a rookery alongside the Great Egrets and Snowy Egrets. The male and female are easy to differentiate because the female displays a tan neck and upper breast while the male's neck is very dark and shiny. Color descriptions vary, and, like other birds, can appear different shades based on the angle and intensity of the sunlight, but black is a good general description. Both the male and female Anhinga display the blue lores around their eyes as the spring mating season approaches. The male begins

Yes, she ignored the sign and is now drying her wings after diving beneath the surface of the lagoon to hunt for fish to feed her chicks in the adjoining rookery.

the courtship by circling overhead at a fairly high altitude and then gliding down to obtain sticks to mark the nesting territory and to initiate the nest construction. He will soar, call and display and gather more sticks to attract a female. She will do the actual construction of the nest, which then becomes the pair's mating site. Two or three days after mating the first egg will be deposited. Mating will continue until she has laid three to six eggs in the nest.

Both Anhinga parents will share the 25 to 30 day incubation. The chicks start out bald, but grow their tan feathers in a few days. The tan down feathers get replaced by molting; in two weeks, the chicks are white for a short time and then, one week later, the true feathers appear. Once again, the chicks will become a light tan. As the young mature, darker brown feathers appear. The older juveniles will achieve their final adult plumage in two to three years, at which time they will begin to contribute to the continuation of the species by carrying out the instinctive mating behaviors inherited from their parents.

Unable to fly, but still capable of escaping danger. Anhinga chicks will jump into the water below their nest until the danger has passed and then they will climb the tree and get back into the nest. A remarkable achievement.

Belted Kingfisher
Megaceryle alcyon

Up to this point you have seen some Lowcountry marsh and lagoon birds that wade, some that swim and others that dive beneath the surface to capture their prey. You also realize that, in nature, there is a wide variety of hunting strategies. If you see this next bird perched in a tree, or on some other structure, you may think that it does not even belong with the other marsh and lagoon birds you've seen so far, but, its name tells you that it does. This is the Belted Kingfisher. And yes, it uses yet another hunting technique to get its food from the Lowcountry water. Rather than wading or going beneath the water to hunt, it sits on a perch overlooking the water, and when it spots a fish near the surface, it rapidly flies to it and either plunges in to capture it or hovers above the water and reaches with that relatively large beak to grab a meal.

Another reason it may appear out of place is that it lacks the long legs and neck of the wading birds and is only about the size of the smaller songbirds we are all familiar with. The Belted Kingfisher is about one foot long from the tip of its beak to the end of its tail feathers. The wings reach almost 2 feet from tip to tip. Often times you will hear the Kingfisher before you see it. Almost every time it launches into flight, it makes its distinctive, rapid and repetitive, call.

The Belted Kingfisher is one of the few species in which the female is more colorful than the male. She possesses the rufous belt around her upper breast that is not seen in the male.

When you do see the Belted Kingfisher, you must remember that, unlike most bird species, the female is the more colorful of the two. She has the distinctive reddish orange, or rufous, belt not seen in the adult male. Both sexes, when juvenile, may display some of this color in their belt, but it is a clear identifying feature of the adult female.

Nesting is another behavior that makes the Belted Kingfisher different from the other marsh and lagoon birds. The mating season begins after the Belted Kingfishers have left the Lowcountry, where some spend the colder months, and have migrated to the northern United States and into Canada where the potential parents use their special fused toes to shovel soil and tunnel into a bank near their feeding grounds. These small birds may dig into the soil for as much as 8 feet. The tunnel slants upward as they proceed so that floodwaters will not reach the five to eight chicks nesting at the inner end of the tunnel. Yet another interesting adaptation provided by one of nature's marvelous creatures. Both Belted Kingfisher parents will share the incubation of the eggs and feeding of the young. The Belted Kingfisher will claim an area of about one half mile along the bank and waterway and defend it from intrusion by other Kingfishers, but, interestingly, they do not mind when other species want to share their tunnel for their nest site as well. One tunnel may have chambers dug out along its walls for use by other birds.

Here is a rare instance where human activity has helped a species. Road excavation and mining have actually produced more exposed banks of soil that the Belted Kingfishers need for their nesting site. This has allowed the Belted Kingfisher population to remain fairly stable over the past several years.

This male Belted Kingfisher launches himself from a favorite perch once he has spotted a fish near the surface. The relatively large beak increases his chance of a successful catch.

DUCKS

Ring-necked Duck

Wood Duck

Canvasback Duck

Redhead Duck

Ruddy Duck

Lesser Scaup

Hooded Merganser

Bufflehead

Ring-necked Duck
Aythya collaris

I MENTIONED PREVIOUSLY that some of the Lowcountry marsh and lagoon birds spend the entire year here, and can be observed year round, while others are only temporary visitors spending the cooler months here before flying north to breed. The Ring-necked Duck is one example of the birds that are here for a relatively short period of time. When their summer habitat, in the northern US and into Canada, gets so cold that ice covers the ponds, the wildfowl species are forced to fly south to find open water in which to feed. In fact, the Ring-necked Ducks fly the farthest of any ducks in their group, known as the diving ducks. There are, of course, many species of birds that travel much greater distances and fly continuously for long periods of time. Whether migrating a few thousand miles, or only a few hundred, both require extraordinary stamina. Of all of the numerous animal groups, only the birds and mammals have a four-chambered heart for more efficient transport of oxygen to their cells. But, the birds have an additional advantage; their lung design allows for a constant absorption of oxygen into their blood so that the energy required for flight, which is about thirteen times their resting need, can remain at an optimal level. The diving ducks, in general, have relatively small wings so they are more maneuverable under water, but this means that, while flying, they need to flap them considerably faster than other birds in order to maintain adequate lift and sustain flight. When the

The white ring around this drake's bill is distinctive, but it is the ring around his neck that gives this species its name.

Above: The female Ring-necked Duck shows her plumage; it's not as colorful as the male's below, but it is still very attractive.

daylight hours become sufficiently long in the early spring, the Ring-necked Duck will take off from a Lowcountry lagoon for the last time and start its migration to the north.

In a pond far north of our coastal plain, the Ring-necked hens and drakes will pair up for mating, but the female will then be the sole nest builder and egg incubator. She will lay about ten eggs in a nest made of grasses and down feathers. Often, the nest will simply float about in the water as the female tends to the eggs for 25 to 29 days. Within a day or two of hatching, the chicks will leave the nest and begin eating both vegetation and aquatic invertebrates. The mother keeps the young hidden in the grasses and may gather them to brood with her at night. In about seven weeks the chicks will have developed their flight feathers and become independent.

Adult Ring-necked Ducks are primarily plant eaters, except when the female is nesting, at which time she will have an omnivorous diet. They are known as diving ducks, and have been known to go down 40 feet, but they will also dabble; that is, they simply stick their head under water to eat available vegetation.

If you get a chance to observe the Ring-necked Ducks in one of the Lowcountry lagoons you will, undoubtedly, recognize them by the ring around their blue-gray beak rather than by the ring around their neck, but with the aid of binoculars, or a camera lens, you may see the distinctive deep magenta feathers circling the base of a black neck. This is another very attractive species gracing the Lowcountry, if only for a brief time each year.

Ring-necked Ducks are diving ducks, but here, two drakes are dabbling, or feeding from the surface, because their food supply is plentiful.

Wood Duck
Aix sponsa

Considered the most beautifully plumed of all North American ducks the Wood Duck is both a migratory species and a permanent resident depending on where the flock calls home. Those in the north have to migrate prior to the winter freeze, but those in the Lowcountry latitudes can remain year round. The Wood Duck gets its name because they nest in the woods. In fact, they do not build nests in the trees, but use natural cavities in the trees themselves as their nests. When storms break a limb off the tree trunk the unprotected wood is subject to decay and a cavity can develop. Wood Ducks also possess special claws on their feet which allow them to perch on tree branches so they are truly arboreal, but also use the lakes, lagoons and marshes as their habitat. They feed by dabbling in the water and eat a variety of vegetation including seeds and fruits. They also don't hesitate to walk on dry land in search for food when necessary. Another good example of interspecies relationships is provided by the Wood Duck and the Beaver. Where

As with most birds, the Wood Duck female is not as colorful as the male, but still presents a striking appearance.

Beavers have made a comeback in their population growth so has the Wood Duck. Beavers make dams out of tree branches in streams. Once dammed, the stream creates a lake, often in wooded areas. This makes an ideal habitat for the Wood Duck; water for feeding and trees for roosting and nesting.

Wood Ducks also faced extinction in the early 1900's because of the fashion craze in plumed hats. Their brilliant colors were prized as were the pure white of the Egrets. Again, concerned citizens and legislation saved a species. People are still helping in many areas because they have constructed Wood Duck nest boxes in places where development has removed stands of trees.

As you know, the male Wood Duck gets his most beautiful plumage during the mating season. When ready to mate the hen will waggle her beak from side to side and the drake will raise his tail and wings and tilt his head back until the two join in mutual preening. Once bonded, those who were raised in the north will migrate to the breeding grounds there. When they arrive, the female will fly up to a tree cavity and the male will follow. He waits while she goes in and inspects their potential nest. If satisfactory, which, in some cases, means it may be way above the forest floor so that predators will have difficulty reaching it, she will line it with her own plucked down feathers and then lay close to a dozen eggs. If nesting sites are scarce a female Wood Duck will lay her eggs in another Wood Duck nest. Incubation can be from 28 to 37 days but, if there are too many eggs, it may harm both clutches because none of the eggs can be incubated successfully.

One of your first science lessons you learned in school was that, due to gravity, all objects, whether a rock or a feather, will fall to earth at the same speed—if there is no air resistance. Fortunately for the Wood Duck chicks there is plenty of air resistance for a tiny bird covered in fluffy feathers because their instinct calls for them to use their special claws to climb to the edge of the nest cavity and jump when they are just one day old. As I said, this may be from a great height, sometimes even over 100 feet. The mother waits on the ground and calls to them, but does not aid them as they fall or as they march to the water which may also be a considerable distance. A little different start to life in northern lakes or Lowcountry waters than you have seen in the previous species pictured.

Wood Ducks are usually pictured in their full mating plumage. Here, you can see them as they appear during the much longer non-breeding period and the way you are more likely to see them here in the Lowcountry.

The drake Wood Duck displaying its late season mating plumage is considered the most attractive of all male ducks.

Male, or drake, Canvasback Ducks show you their distinctive profile – a gentle slope from their head to the tip of their bill.

Canvasback Duck
Aytha valisineria

An obvious question is: How did these ducks get that name, Canvasback? But, the answer is nothing mysterious. They were named for the simple reason that their backs appear to be the color of canvas. These once plentiful diving ducks are getting increasingly more rare in the Lowcountry because they breed in ponds in the prairie lands of the northern US and into Canada, and this habitat has been changing. The prairie topography was carved out by the last ice age ice sheet, which left many ponds called potholes; but now, much of this land is being altered and used for agriculture, so the Canvasbacks' nesting territory is decreasing. Also, they are more sensitive to temperature fluctuations and pollution than some other species that share their habitat. Canvasback Ducks primarily feed on the roots and tubers of aquatic plants. Because these birds winter in the south, the pollution and fertilizer runoff that has altered the submerged vegetation in the water here in the south has also contributed to the Canvasback Ducks' declining numbers.

If you do see the Canvasbacks, you will notice that they have a very distinctive profile; their beaks slant downward from fairly high on their heads and make more of a straight line slope than is seen in other ducks.

Diving ducks, as well as many other birds and animals, have a special structure called a nictating membrane in their eyes. This can be thought of as a third eyelid; it allows the birds to see well while diving for food, while at the same time, protecting their eyes from physical damage. Canvasback Ducks can dive down to 30 feet if necessary.

As you know, most of the ducks seen in the Lowcountry migrate here in the winter when conditions are too difficult in the north. The Canvasback has the distinction of being the fastest migratory duck, and has been known to cover as much as 70 miles in an hour. When they return to their nesting territory, each hen will lay 7 to 9 large green eggs in a large reed nest. (Other species may also lay their eggs in the Canvasback Duck's nest, which is another contributing factor to their population decline.)

The downy chicks hatch after the typical 3 to 4 week incubation period. They leave the nest quite quickly and start feeding on aquatic vegetation. Both sexes start out with yellow eyes, but in about three months, their eyes will begin to turn red. The young mature rapidly, and when just one year old, they will be considered adults with the hens being about 19 inches long and the drakes about 20 inches. By the time they return to the north after their first winter in the Lowcountry, they will be mature enough to participate in the mating process.

Redhead Duck
Aythya americana

I know—there's no need to explain how this diving duck got the name Redhead. Unfortunately, I could repeat the same information about its population decline that I shared with you regarding the Canvasback Duck. Redheads are even more dependent on specific aquatic vegetation species, which have declined for the reasons I mentioned previously, as well as by being depleted by an increase in fish populations that have expanded their range into the duck's breeding grounds.

The Redhead Duck is considered medium sized at about 19 inches in length. As with many other ducks, these are in the Lowcountry for the winter months, but migrate to their northern mating territory in the early spring. They do not stay with their mates from the previous year, but seek new mates as winter turns to spring. The male bends his head backward until his bill touches his back near his tail to gain a female's attention. She replies by holding her head high and making a 'yes' up and down movement with her bill.

Many, but certainly not all, marsh and lagoon birds show their dimorphism, or two different plumages, displayed by the male and female. As seen in the majority of bird species, the male Redhead Duck is more colorful.

An interesting behavior that adds to their population decline is the habit of many Redhead Duck hens laying their eggs in other ducks' nests. If this manner of egg depositing is not timed correctly, there is a good chance that the Redhead Duck eggs will not be incubated for the necessary time and the eggs will be lost. When the hen has laid her eggs, she is abandoned by the drake. He will then molt and lose his flight feathers and have to wait about one month before being able to fly again.

The chicks will also take about ten weeks to develop their flight feathers. Both sexes have the blue bill and feet, and both will become mature adults their first year; but only the drakes will display the red head that gives this most attractive bird its name.

You can see that female Redhead Ducks easily blend in with the lagoon vegetation, important when nesting in the north so that she, and her nest, are less apparent to predators.

Her flock is sharing the Lowcountry lagoon with a small flock of Ring-necked Ducks.

Ruddy Duck
Oxyura jamaicensis

When you see Ruddy Ducks in the Lowcountry, it will be in the late fall or early winter, and they may not be all that ruddy, or red, in color. They, like most of the birds you have seen, display their colors in the spring and then lose their colored plumage after the mating season. Some Ruddy Ducks may still have vestiges of the ruddy red body feathers, while others may have already changed completely.

I have no proof, but the appearance of the Ruddy Duck's bill is strong evidence that it was these ducks that were the model for all of those little yellow rubber duckies. That seemingly very wide bill just follows the efficient pattern found in the other duck species' bills. Yes, there is a purpose for that bill design. Whether dabbling or diving, when ducks take a mouthful of food they also get a mouthful of water. The ducks' bills are designed to squeeze water out as the bill is closed. The edges of the bill are designed like a strainer, so that water can be removed before the food is swallowed.

Like the other diving ducks, the Ruddy Duck's legs are positioned well to the rear of its body. This, too, is an anatomical feature of the diving ducks because it allows them to tip forward, or dive head first, more easily using propulsion from their webbed feet. In fact, the Ruddy Duck has its feet farther back than most all of the other diving ducks. Efficient in the water, this design makes it nearly impossible for these ducks to travel on land. Because they are so 'front heavy' they cannot maintain their balance when out of the water. As with the other diving ducks, the Ruddy Duck's wings are small, which

means it also has to use its legs to run on the water, or patter, to gain flying speed.

The Ruddy Duck is one of the smaller species at only about 15 inches long. This includes the tail, which is considered long compared to other duck tails. While these ducks are swimming, the tail is frequently held high, and it is also used as a display during the mate attraction season.

Besides the fading of the ruddy color, the male's all-white cheek feathers displayed for courtship may diminish substantially, and the male may come close to resembling a female late in the year, but he will lack the horizontal dark line through the cheek that marks the female. In the spring, the Ruddy Ducks will return to the north, drakes will develop the red, ruddy color, mate and build a nest in dense marsh grasses. Unlike most ducks, the Ruddy Duck drakes and hens may form pair bonds that last for a few years.

If you look closely you can see that the red, ruddy, breeding color is fading away. In many species male ducks go through an 'eclipse' phase – an extensive loss of breeding plumage. They even lose some of their flight feathers for a time.

The Lesser Scaup and a smaller female Bufflehead Duck may spend a few weeks in the Lowcountry before migrating when the northern lake ice melts in the spring.

LESSER SCAUP
Aythya affinis

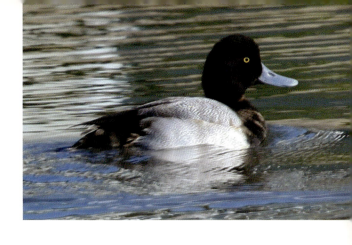

Yes, there is a Greater Scaup as well, and it's just a little bit larger than the Lesser Scaup, which is about 17 inches overall in length. Also, the Lesser Scaup has a bit more of a peak to its head crown, while the Greater Scaup's head profile is more rounded. Both Scaup species, like most of the ducks seen in the Lowcountry, are northern birds, except when it's necessary for them to migrate south to find open water for feeding. In the north, they may be seen in large flocks, or "rafts," as they're called when they're on the water and made up of thousands of other Scaups. The Greater Scaup is found in salt water whereas the Lesser Scaup prefers freshwater lakes and must move to the south when the northern lakes freeze.

Scaups are diving ducks and will eat larva, small mollusks and other invertebrates as well as aquatic plants.

Back in their northern breeding grounds, the hens will lay 8 to 10 eggs each in a down-lined, bowl-shaped grass nest and will incubate them with no assistance from the drake Lesser Scaup. After the 21 to 27 day incubation period, the chicks will hatch and immediately attempt diving for their own food. But, their just dried downy chick feathers make them quite buoyant, so they pop to the surface quickly. However, within a few weeks the chicks will be able to stay under water for nearly 30 seconds. In about 50 days, they will develop their mature 29-inch wings and be able to fly.

As you know, the Killdeer pretends to be injured to lure predators away from its nest or young. Well, the Lesser Scaup goes one step further and pretends to be dead—not to protect the young, but to fool a fox hunting for a live bird to capture. If caught, the Lesser Scaup will go limp in the fox's mouth in hopes that the fox will drop it, wondering why the bird is not panicked as is usually the case with other captured prey. Apparently, this behavior has met with enough success that the instinct has been passed on through many generations; it is now part of the Lesser Scaup's genetic makeup.

I feel I would be remiss if I did not tell you how the Scaup got its name; it's certainly not a term found in common usage. It is believed that the word Scaup is derived from both the old French word, *escalope,* and the old Dutch, *schelpe,* both referring to mollusks, which are the soft-bodied animals such as clams, snails, and squid. Because mollusks make up much of the Scaup's diet, over the years, this descriptive term has become its official name. In some regions, the Lesser Scaup may be called the Blue Bill, for obvious reasons.

Hooded Merganser
Lophodytes cucullatus

The Hooded Merganser is another small diving duck and is more prevalent in the Lowcountry lagoons during the winter months than most of the other ducks. It is a duck because it has the webbed feet seen in the other duck species, but its sub-group, the Mergansers, is distinguished by the narrow, pointed and serrated beaks they have in place of the broad flat bill you have seen on the other ducks. The serrated edges allow the Hooded Mergansers to grasp small fish and other aquatic invertebrates they pursue while diving.

As you have seen with some other marsh and lagoon birds, there is a big change in appearance between the juvenile Hooded Mergansers and the adults. Both sexes, as adults, have the ability to raise their head crest feathers to signal to other members of the flock which is usually composed of about a dozen birds. This species breeds in the northern US and into Canada. The male displays his crest and flaps his wings to attract a female. She responds by pointing her beak skyward and bobbing her head. After mating she will begin laying six to twelve eggs in the nest located in a hole in a tree. The

drake's reproductive role ceases after fertilization and the hen is left to incubate the eggs for about 30 days. Within 24 hours of hatching the mother leads the chicks to water where they begin their search for food. They will spend about ten weeks swimming and diving before they develop their flight wings and are able to fly. Soon, they will be full grown at about 18 inches in length and in about a year they will start the transition from the bland camouflage colors seen in the juveniles into the striking plumage of the adult Hooded Mergansers.

Top: The yellow bill of the immature female Hooded Merganser contrasts with the dark bill of the young male. He may show the striking appearance of the mature male when he returns to the Lowcountry next year.

BUFFLEHEAD DUCK
Bucephala albeola

THE BUFFLEHEAD has a unique distinction; at only a little more than a foot long, it is the smallest North American diving duck. When the male, with a large white patch on its head, fluffs its head feathers, his head appears to be too large for his small body. Because a Buffalo's head, with its horns and hair, looks large compared to its body, people started calling this little duck a Buffalo Head. Over the years, it contracted to Bufflehead.

Being small has its advantages and disadvantages. The advantage for the Bufflehead becomes evident during the spring nesting season. Like the Wood Ducks, the Buffleheads nest in tree cavities created by decay, insects and woodpeckers. In years gone by, a large Bufflehead required a large hole in the tree, and raccoons or weasels could get in to steal the eggs; meanwhile, a small Bufflehead could occupy a small cavity, and some predators couldn't gain access. Over time, more small Bufflehead progeny survived during the nesting period, so Buffleheads passing on genes for smaller bodies predominated. Now the Bufflehead population is comprised of these successful small ducks.

The disadvantage has to do with the energy requirements of various sized warm-blooded animals. Small warm-blooded animals have more surface area, skin, compared to their body mass than do large warm-blooded animals. Because heat radiates out through the skin, small animals have to burn many more calories, relative to their size, in order to maintain their body temperature. Buffleheads, being small, and spending much of their time in cool water, must eat frequently in order to burn enough calories to keep their inter-

Small Bufflehead ducks must make frequent dives to search for food so that they can consume the calories required to keep their internal temperature at its optimum.

nal temperature within the proper range. This means nearly constant diving and eating for the Bufflehead, whereas the larger ducks can afford to rest and even sleep while floating in a marsh or lagoon. Adult Buffleheads will take turns watching for potential predators while the other members of the usually quite small flock dive and eat. They are primarily carnivorous and consume insects and other aquatic invertebrates, but they will eat plant material as well.

Buffleheads are monogamous, and the pairs return to the same nesting area each spring with fairly accurate timing. They will arrive each year on nearly the same date as in previous years. The hens will lay from a half dozen to nearly a dozen eggs and incubate them for about thirty days. And, as with the Wood Duck, the day after hatching the Bufflehead chicks will leap from the tree cavity nest and make their way to the water to begin feeding.

In about fifty days, the chicks will fledge and be able to fly to the Lowcountry in the fall so that you can visit a lagoon and enjoy these small, cute ducks.

When there is enough food at the surface, dabbling – rather than diving – may suffice; it is demonstrated by this female Bufflehead.

Pied-billed Grebe
Podilymbus podiceps

Here's another bird with an interesting name, the origin of which you might like to know: Pied-billed Grebe. The name is derived from the coloration of the beak or bill, but here in the Lowcountry you might not always observe the dark band on the beak; it's part of the spring mating display, and not always visible at other times of the year. The term "pied" is derived from the Middle English; it originally referred to the black and white feather colors seen on the Magpie. Now, two-toned beaks, or other features, may simply be called pied.

The Pied-billed Grebe and other Grebes, have their own category because they do not have the true webbed feet of the ducks, but, like the American Coot, have lobes on their toes to aid in swimming. You can also see that their beak is curved at the tip like that of the carnivorous hawks and eagles. It may be hard to picture these small, 13 inch birds as predators, but their diet does consist of small animals found in the marsh and lagoon waters.

Pied-billed Grebes dive for their prey and also to escape danger. When they do fly, it's usually for migration and mostly done at night. Some populations stay in warm areas year round, while the ones from farther north migrate to areas like the Lowcountry and then return to the north in the spring.

The pied (two-toned) bill may be seen here in the south if it is close to breeding time and the birds are ready to migrate to the north. At other times the ring around the bill may be much less distinct.

When they have completed their migration, they will establish a nesting territory and begin gathering vegetation for a floating nest. Both Pied-billed Grebe parents incubate the eggs for 23 to 27 days. Interestingly, the chicks are nearly self sufficient within an hour of hatching. They will ride and sleep on a parent's back for ten days or so, and then stay close by for another two months. At the end of this period of time they will gain their total independence.

OSPREY
Pandion haliaetus

All raptors have extraordinary vision which allows them to see prey from far away. Once they spot a potential meal, they dive rapidly and then grasp it with their sharp talons.

SO FAR YOU HAVE SEEN some Lowcountry marsh and lagoon birds that hunt while wading and others that get their food while swimming or diving. Whether their beak is straight, curved, hooked, or flattened like a duck's bill, the one thing that they all have in common is that, in order to eat, they must gather food with their beak. You have seen the great variety that nature provides and, yes, there is even more. Another type of bird, instead of using a beak or bill to catch prey, uses the sharp curved talons on the toes of its feet to grasp fish directly from the water or, in some cases, animals from land. These birds are known as raptors.

I stated that a purpose of this book was to show you birds that are not usually seen at the shore, but the Osprey—the only raptor that plunges feet first into water—is an exception. In fact, the Osprey is also known as the Seahawk, because it not only hunts for fish in the marsh and lagoon waters, but also from the ocean. So you may see the Osprey, the Seahawk, either at the shore or in a marsh or lagoon. Another commonly used term for the Osprey is Fish Hawk. You may hear its piercing call before seeing it as it circles above the water and uses its excellent vision to see a fish near the surface. Once a fish is spotted, the Osprey will quickly dive toward the water and then, uniquely, plunge feet first into the water. An anatomical feature seen in Ospreys is their ability to turn one toe so that they can hold a fish with two talons on each side for a sure grip. If a dive is successful, the bird will fly up, pause for a moment to shake off the excess water, turn the fish so that it's head first, for aerodynamic purposes, and then continue to a

nest to feed chicks, or to a roosting spot to tear apart the fish for its own consumption.

Ospreys nest in a high perch. It may be a tree or any appropriate platform, either natural or a structure made by humans. The same nest site may be used year after year by an Osprey pair. The male will arrive at the nest site a few days before the female. He will then fly up, hover and then dive. This behavior, to establish his territory and to signal the female, is repeated numerous times. Once the female arrives and the two pair up, the male will start the construction, or reconstruction, of the nest; and when both adults, which have the same appearance, find it satisfactory, the female will lay two to five eggs, which will incubate for a quite lengthy 37-40 days. Naturally, the egg

Above: These three Osprey chicks are nearly ready to leave the nest for the first time. Below: At just a few weeks old, hungry young chicks await their next meal.

laid first will hatch first and the oldest chick, with a head start on its younger siblings, will be able to get the majority of fish delivered by the male parent that does all of the fishing for the chicks while the female broods them. If he cannot keep up with the demand from all of the chicks, the younger, weaker ones will starve. Again, that's the way nature works. It's insurance that at least one offspring survives to carry on the species.

Osprey chicks look very similar to the adults, so the best way to know their maturity level is to watch and see if they can fly or if they are only able to flap their wings, but not get airborne. They start practicing flight at three to four weeks and fledge at about two months. Two weeks after their first flights, they will follow their father to the fishing grounds, and in another month, they will be on their own. When they are full grown, they will be 23 inches tall and

have a wingspan of 4½ to 6 feet. However, it will be three years before they reach sexual maturity.

These large, majestic birds have been a very successful species and can be seen soaring and hunting for fish around the globe. Ospreys from the cold north migrate all the way to South America each winter. Here in the Lowcountry, there is no need for them to migrate, so you can admire them year round.

Beautiful in flight, efficient while hunting and a very successful species. Let's ensure that they will have plenty of pristine waters so that they can continue to catch enough fish to maintain a healthy population.

Bald Eagle
Haliaeetus leucocephalus

THE BALD EAGLE is another raptor that uses its talons to capture fish directly from the water. While soaring, or flying at up to 65 miles per hour, the Eagle's fantastic vision can spot a fish near the water's surface from a substantial height. The Bald Eagle can then dive toward the water at nearly 200 miles per hour. Once near the surface it glides with its talons extended and deftly grasps the fish while continuing its glide. It will then continue on, flying to either a nest containing chicks to feed or to a perch, where it will use the sharp, strong, curved beak to tear apart its freshly caught meal. Bald Eagles not only capture fish, but will also hunt other birds, steal food from another Eagle or scavenge carrion upon occasion.

The Bald Eagle became our nation's symbol in 1782, at which time there were an estimated 500,000 Bald Eagles in what are now the 48 contiguous states. By the 1960s, there were only 1,000 Bald Eagles left in this vast area. Part of their population decline was due to the fact that hunting them was encouraged, since it was believed that they killed livestock. But, the major reason for their near extinction was not hunting, but something entirely new. The creation of chemical pesticides appeared to be wonderful development for humans because it dramatically increased crop yield; this was needed to feed a growing world population. Unfortunately, these new chemicals also ended up being washed into our nation's lakes and rivers. Once there, they became incorporated into aquatic plants and small animals. Each larger and larger animal that consumed the smaller animals in the food chain received a higher

and higher dose of these chemicals. The pesticides became very concentrated in the larger fish: the same fish that the Bald Eagles consumed. The chemical pesticides did not seem to affect the adult Eagles directly, but when the female Bald Eagles laid their eggs, the egg shells were so thin and weak that the eggs broke when an adult attempted to incubate them. Here was one more lesson in the complexity of nature's food webs and how our seemingly innocent actions can have drastic effects. Once again, but almost too late, people took action, and the Bald Eagle population is now estimated at 20,000. This was a lesson we must all learn from, never forget and never repeat.

Bald Eagles do not get their majestic appearance until they are four or five years old. Once mature, they may be as large as 42 inches and have a wing span of nearly 8 feet. Some Bald Eagles have been documented to live 40 years.

Once mature, a Bald Eagle pair will fly to a fairly high altitude, grasp onto each other's feet and tumble toward the ground in uncontrolled, rolling flight. At the last possible moment, they will let go of each other and recover controlled flight—an unusual courtship activity, for sure. The pair will then continue to prepare for becoming parents. A large nest, often added to year after year, will be constructed in a tall tree. Once the nest is ready, the female will lay one to three eggs. When they hatch, the light gray chicks will be attended to and fed by both parents. In about nine weeks, the chicks will be full grown, but they may not leave the nest for another week or two. The now brown-plumed chicks will stay near the nest and hunt with the parents for about six weeks and then go off to perfect their own hunting skills. The juveniles may travel extensively

Although quite large, this Bald Eagle chick was still unable to fly and stayed near the nest while a parent patiently stood guard. Just days later the chick soared off to begin its new life in the Lowcountry.

for the next four years and then find a life long mate and do their part in producing more of these marvelous examples of wildlife that you are fortunate enough to find here hunting for fish in our Lowcountry marsh and lagoon water.

While enjoying pictures of these marsh and lagoon birds, you have also patiently read about some wildlife conservation concerns I hope you share with me. Now, please bear with me for a bit longer. I was a biology teacher for many years, and I want to present one more lesson about all of those funny sounding italicized terms you have seen. I'm aware that you know they are the scientific names for each of the various bird species you have seen, but I think you might enjoy learning a little more information about the use of these two word Latin terms. Do you remember your biology classes? Carl von Linne (Carl Linnaeus, 1707-1778) started our modern system of naming living things by giving them a genus and species name in Latin. We still use his binomial nomenclature today.

For example, *Boa constrictor* is both the common and scientific name for a very large snake. *Gorilla gorilla* needs no explanation. All house cats are *Felis domestica*, domesticated felines. *Felis leo* gave us Leo the lion, and you don't need help with *Felis tigris*.

In Latin, you, and all humans, are *Homo sapien*. Greek is also an origin of many modern words, so this can, at times, lead to confusion. In Latin, *homo* refers to man, but from the ancient Greek it refers to things that are the same. You are *homoeothermic*—warm-blooded—which means you maintain the same body temperature. Some of us remember when milk came with the cream floating on top of the milk, instead of being all blended together, or *homogenized*—all the same—as it is today. This is why scientists all use Latin for naming plants and animals; so there is no confusion about the name or what it means.

The Bald Eagle is *Haliaeetus leucocephalus* around the world, no matter what language the scientist may use for everyday speech. *Haliateetus* is Latin for sea eagle and *leucocephalus* can be interpreted if you do, in fact, remember some biology. Our white blood cells are technically *leucocytes*—white cells—and *cephalus* refers to your head. So, the genus and species, in Latin, for the Eagle is Eagle with white head. The use of the name Bald Eagle probably originated from an Old English term, *piebald*, which, as you learned earlier, uses pied to mean two different colors—the brown and white distinctly separated on the adult Bald Eagle's familiar plumage.

I encourage you to spend some time looking up the meaning of some of the other genus and species names I have provided. You will find some of them very interesting, I am sure. Also, please, do some searching for more information about these marsh and lagoon birds, as well as for other species you

may see here in the Lowcountry. The more we all learn about the multitude of organisms that we coexist with, the better we will be able to understand how our actions may affect them and ultimately, us.

Whether you live in the Lowcountry or are a visitor to this fascinating area of the east coast, I hope that you will be able to visit some of the marshes and lagoons so that you can see the amazing birds pictured here, as well as the other wildlife that, I am certain, will provide you with a most enjoyable and rewarding experience.

The white head gave the Eagle its species name and the contrasting brown and white feathers, or piebald plumage, gave it its title, Bald Eagle.

When you see this majestic bird, our nation's symbol, you may experience an emotion unlike anything you feel when you spot the other beautiful Lowcountry birds.

REFERENCES

1. Dunn, J.L., & Alderfer, J. *Field Guide to the Birds of Eastern North America.* Washington D.C: National Geographic.

2. Farrand, J. Jr. (1988). *An Audubon Handbook Eastern Birds.* New York, N.Y: McGraw-Hill Book Co.

3. Peterson, R.T. (2008). *Peterson Field Guide to Birds of North America.* Boston-New York: Houghton Mifflin Company

4. Peterson, R.T. (1980). *A Field Guide to the Birds.* 4th Ed. Boston, MA: Houghton Mifflin Co.

5. Sibley. D.A. (2000). *The Sibley Guide to Birds.* NY: Alfred A. Knoph

6. http://en.wikepedia.org

7. http://identifywhatbird.com

8. http://www.allaboutbirds.org